DEALING WITH DIVORCE IN ILLINOIS

USEFUL INFO THAT MAY BE HELPFUL IN YOUR CASE

Ronald L. Bell, Esq.

ISBN: 978-1-941645-81-9

Designed and Published by:
Speakeasy Publications
73-03 Bell Blvd, #10
Oakland Gardens, NY 11364
www.SpeakeasyMarketingInc.com
(888) 225-8594

DISCLAIMER

This publication is intended to be informational only. No legal advice is being given, and no attorney-client relationship is intended to be created by reading this material. If you are facing legal issues, whether criminal or civil, seek professional legal counsel to get your questions answered.

Ronald L. Bell & Associates P.C.
1113 S. Milwaukee Ave., Suite 204
Libertyville, IL 60048
(847) 495-6000
www.bestlakecountylawyer.com

Testimonials

As with most divorces I suspect things get tense and a bit confusing going through the process. But Ronald was there with me every step of the way when I needed him. He and his highly trained staff are easy to work with, really know their business. Ronald supports his clients and keeps his client's interest as his top priority. This made a very difficult situation much easier and understandable. Thank goodness he was on my side and not on the other side. I would highly recommend Ronald and his team should someone require their services. **- John**

Ronald brought notable care and attention to the particular needs and dynamic of our family circumstances. Creative and insightful in addressing our challenges, he presented us with multiple options and painstakingly explained the implications of each. With his guidance, we felt well equipped to make a series of informed legal decisions and take the steps needed to protect our interests. We would return without hesitation. **- Stephen**

I wanted to write this review for my outstanding attorney Ronald Bell. Ron was able to turn a very unpleasant divorce into a manageable divorce. I was able to work side by side with Ron and his team of professionals throughout this whole experience. It was truly a pleasure working with Ron and Doreen. Ron helped me along through this whole process from A-Z, in the office as well as in court. Thanks again for all your help. If you're looking for an attorney, Ron's your man. **- Todd**

Ron is very aggressive and knowledgeable. When getting divorced, do as he says it's only in your best interest even if you don't like what he has to say. I got everything I wanted even after at times I wanted to give up he still fought for me. The day of my divorce waiting outside the court room waiting my turn, Ron approached another attorney and started arguing for a different client of his so that showed me that his clients are always on his mind. Thank you again Ron. **- A Divorce Client**

"I got married while I was on active duty and got out and joined my local reserve unit out here. When my former spouse asked for a divorce I had a week before I had to go out of state for almost a year to find a good divorce lawyer. I came across Ron on a Google search and met up with him and explained everything that was going on. While I was away he made every attempt to answer my phone calls and answer any questions I had and kept my mind at ease with the whole process. He really knows what he's doing and will be very up front with you. I have nothing but good things to say about him and would recommend him to friends or family." **- Zachary**

"Words can't express all the appreciation we have for Ron and Doreen. I must say that if you are looking for a great Lawyer, look no further – Ron is it. They go above and beyond of what is expected. I highly recommend Ron. You will not regret your decision on choosing him. Ron and Doreen thank you for all you did." **- Gabriela**

Table Of Contents

Attorney Ronald Bell owns the law firm of Ronald Bell & Associates, a general practice firm concentrating on divorce. A college graduate at the age of 20, he went on to attend law school, graduating at the age of 23. Attorney Bell went before the Supreme Court when he was 24 and has been practicing law for 37 years. As an Assistant Attorney General, he was handpicked to argue a case before Chief Justice Rehnquist. Attorney Bell was also handpicked to argue five cases in front of the Illinois Supreme Court on behalf of the State of Illinois.

Attorney Bell has also handled hundreds of appeals for the State of Illinois, many habeas corpus petitions and has represented many other state agencies. He was also the "Bingo" prosecutor and went after the mafia on behalf of the State of Illinois. When Attorney Bell left the Attorney General's office, he went into private practice and began handling medical malpractice cases. He won over $4 million right off-the-bat on a case and soon after, became corporate counsel to what became a very large company after Attorney Bell's arrival. In fact, he helped them grow to $250 million gross revenue and they are now a major consulting company. He was in constant litigation with competitors for their employees and litigated cases for 20 years in many states, including San Francisco and Texas. He is actually nationally known as a result of that.

Throughout this whole time, from the time Attorney Bell left the Attorney General's office, he was doing divorce work as well.

Knowledge Of Community And His Peers

Attorney Ronald Bell knows the community; he knows the judges and practices before them all. He finds it is very important to know the judges as they are the ultimate decision makers. Like every marriage, every judge is different. Judges have different quirks and different ways of doing things that an attorney needs to be familiar with if one is to be successful.

Some judges want to hear certain facts; other judges want to hear other facts. Some judges will make a prompt decision and some will take hours to do so. Knowing who you are dealing with is just as important in many cases as knowing the law. You don't want to stumble when you should have been arguing something in a different way before a particular judge. Attorney Bell brings that kind of experience to the table.

It's important to understand that because most marriages end in divorce today, people oftentimes don't know where to turn. They look for a friend or for a relative to advise them where to go. If it's more of a private matter, they may not want anyone to know their business and they often go to the internet to see what they can find to educate themselves about. There's nothing wrong with that. However, going with a proven divorce attorney who has tried thousands of cases and who has limited himself to only taking on what he wants to work on, is much better than taking a chance on a hit or a miss from an internet source or solely relying on someone else's experience.

Attorney Bell is rated 10 out of 10 on AVVO and is a member of the National Association of Distinguished Counsel; an organization that includes many famous attorneys where you have to be nominated by your peers, are seriously vetted and only then are you officially nominated. Just one percent of the United States attorneys can be in this organization, so it quite an honor and accomplishment.

Attorney Bell is also a member of the American Academy of Trial Lawyers Association and has been rated as one of the top 112 attorneys in the state of Illinois. He was also rated as Top 10 Best Family Lawyers by the American Academy of Family Law Attorneys. He has also been named in the National Associates Top 100 as well as in the top 100 best attorneys in Illinois.

Attorney Bell knows that an attorney who deals in family law has to be a jack of many trades. Believe it or not, many attorneys are not. He has experience in real estate closings, is a title agent and represents the Chicago Title & Trust Company, the largest trust company for real estate closings in the country. This is important because there are many real estate issues in a divorce that can come up; refinance, sale and short sales issues are just a few.

Attorney Bell has also handled and won many jury trials in personal injury cases. For example, if you are representing a disabled person in a divorce case or a person with a handicap, you need to understand and interpret medical information in order to proceed in a case to help a client achieve their result; to know what their rights are and to understand their disabilities.

If you happen to be representing the other person, then you may have to know if their disability is real and what their limitations are. These all can be part of a divorce case. You have to be somewhat of a psychiatrist and compassionate to your client because their whole world is going topsy-turvy. For the first time in their life, they don't know what's up and what's down. They just know that they are not happy in a situation.

ACHIEVEMENTS & AWARDS

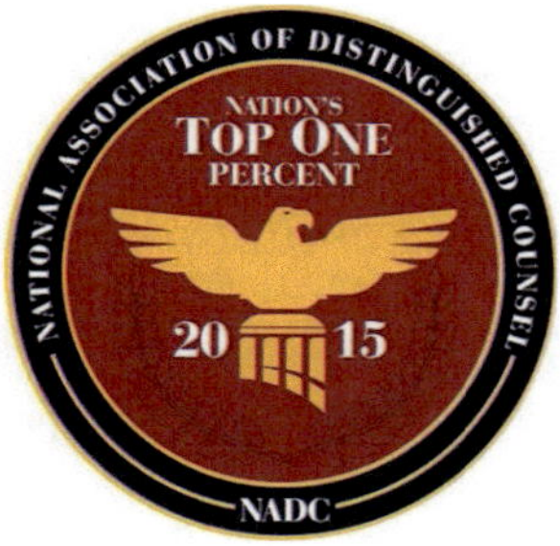

General Reasons For Divorce In Illinois

Fifty percent of all marriages in the United States end in divorce. When you put two people together they may have the same idea of leading a blissful life but they have different ways of going about doing it which conflict with each other. When you get to a point in a marriage where you are contemplating divorce, you need a skilled attorney who engages in that kind of thing. A skilled attorney keeps up with the law and is able to know where the case is going, where the case has been and can predict the outcome with a degree of relative accuracy.

Usually the threshold question Attorney Bell asks his clients is, "If your husband or your wife is not going to change, do you see yourself being in this marriage for a longer period of time? The answer is normally "No. I don't see myself in this marriage if nothing's going to change."

At that point most people commit to go forward with the divorce. However, just because the parties are going to file for divorce does not necessarily mean they are going to get divorced. Many people actually reconcile.

Once a couple files for divorce one of two things generally happens; either the person they file against agrees divorce is the right step and they move forward or that same person gets down on their hands and knees and wants to work it out. In the latter case, the couple usually would go to counseling and give it a good six months while the divorce is pending to see if they can reconcile. When that happens, it's a wonderful thing because people often say their relationship is now what they always wanted it to be and it's better than ever. So alas, divorce can cure a bad marriage! However, divorce can also cure a bad marriage by dissolving it.

The Role Of A Prenuptial Agreement In A Divorce Case

Many people enter into prenuptial agreements nowadays. Attorney Bell sees and drafts a good number of them himself. It is a statement that has to be well balance and each side must disclose all assets to make it fair. Usually it's if you're married 2 years, you get X amount of dollars; if you're married for 4 years, you get X amount of dollars; six years, X amount of dollars and so on and so forth.

However, prenuptial agreements have volumes of litigation against them. It really comes down to how they were drafted and what the circumstances are. In all actuality, nearly half are held invalid.

For example, would you expect a prenuptial agreement to still be valid when years down the road there are now three children and you acquired a business during the marriage? Most likely not. There are issues with prenuptial agreements in that they are not as solid as people want to think they are.

That being said, it can be a good thing to have a prenuptial agreement. It's a contract and if there is nothing unusual about the case, the courts will usually enforce such a contract and will hold it valid. When you walk into a divorce case, it could save you a lot of money and attorney's fees on both sides as well as a lot of aggravation.

> Prenuptial agreements have volumes of litigation against them. It really comes down to how they were drafted and what the circumstances are. In all actuality, nearly half are held invalid.

Impact Of Changes In Illinois Family Law Statutes On Divorce Cases

On January 1st of 2016, the law in Illinois changed dramatically. It is the most significant change in over 30 years since 1977. The highlights of that law change are as follows:

There is no more custody and there is no more joint custody. As attorneys in Lake County, Illinois, we always fought about the way the terms were. We had many people just fighting about the term custody or custodian and what that meant.

Now legislation has basically decided to get rid of those terms and replace with allocation of rights or parental rights.

The allocation of parental rights really means both parents have rights. You also may share some mutual rights. It's a much better issue that we deal with today in custody than we did before they embellished the term because now, they have a rule that they want an allocation agreement, or parental rights agreement, within three months of the filing of the case.

If it's not done in 190 days, in Lake County anyway, what they will do is send the parties out to mediation, a process where the parents will talk to an independent mediator appointed by the judge where they will try to reach an agreement.

What has also changed in the law is there are no grounds for divorce anymore in Illinois. They abolished adultery, mental cruelty, physical cruelty, habitual drunkenness for two years and a variety of things. Today, what we have is very simple; no fault divorce. Irreconcilable differences caused an irretrievable breakdown of the marriage, where all attempts of reconciliation have been unsuccessful. Therefore, what we have today is that if you want a divorce, there is no waiting period. You ask for a divorce and you can be divorced. You don't have to prove anything; you just have to ask for it.

What has been consistent in the old law though is that property is considered equitable in Illinois to be usually 50/50; sometimes 60/40, sometimes 55/45. That's really the range of what fairness is in Illinois.

Mediation is where neither party is represented but they want an agreement to be reached. The problem with this procedure is that while it can be very effective, productive and can result in an agreement, the mediator does not care what either side is getting. The mediator only cares about getting an agreement. The question then arises, "Is this agreement in your best interest?"

You should have a skilled attorney review the agreement before signing it. When someone engages in mediation without an attorney, they should be wary of what the agreement will say. They did not hire the mediator and the mediator does not write the agreement. They give a starting point so the attorney can write the agreement as an outline of what they did and try to put everything into the right language. It is very unfair and impartial to both people because you can't have a one-sided agreement and still cover all of your bases.

THE ROLE OF A GUARDIAN AD LITEM IN A CUSTODY PROCEEDING

If mediation fails or if the judge decides not to go to the mediation, he or she will appoint a GAL, a Guardian Ad Litem. A Guardian Ad Litem is an attorney for the child or a child's advocate. This is a person that will represent the child's interest and be the eyes and ears of the court so that the judge can investigate these cases. The GAL often goes out to your house and meets with you and your spouse and the children and advocate what they believe is the best position. Usually the GAL's opinions are followed by the court. It's very important to note that if the GAL's opinion is against your client or is something that the client doesn't like, you can appoint a psychological expert to evaluate the case under the new law as well.

It used to be that you each person would spend a ton of money on two different experts but under the new Illinois law, which has changed dramatically, the judge now has the power to appoint one expert. If this expert clashes with the GAL, usually the GAL will fold and will adopt the professional's psychological opinion. If the GAL doesn't change the opinion, as a court-appointed expert, their investigation goes into evidence with the judge.

It makes the GAL rule as credible if they're clashing with the psychological professional. That's the ultimate finality of a custody battle. What happens is then the judge will make a decision after hearing the testimony of the parties and witnesses as to the best interest of the minor children and the best interest hasn't changed in the law; that still controls.

> A Guardian Ad Litem is an attorney for the child or a child's advocate. This is a person that will represent the child's interest and be the eyes and ears of the court so that the judge can investigate these cases.

Division Of Property During A Divorce In Illinois

In Illinois, we consider property division regardless of fault. The partnership is dissolving and the court will do the best they can to make a fair resolution to both parties. The court looks at contribution and at ability to acquire assets in the future. So for example, when you have a spouse that is a stay-at-home mom, her contribution is considered to be equal to the bread earner who is going out of the home to work; it's equal.

If someone did contribute non-marital money under certain circumstances where it could be traced, they can get that back as a special contribution. If one party owns a piece of property that's non-marital, being defined as acquired before marriage, that is not the subject of a divorce. The judge can't touch it. That is your own property and the judge doesn't have jurisdiction over it. Also gift or inheritance that occurs during marriage can be considered non-marital property too if it's kept separate and apart from the marital money.

Other than that, any property acquired during marriage is marital property regardless of whose name it's in. So his bank account is her bank account, her bank account is his bank account and so on. It doesn't matter in whose name the car is in. It doesn't matter whose bank account number it is. It is part of the whole picture or the whole circle of the marital property.

If something was acquired on the date of marriage and after, it is subject to being split up by the judge equitably; which oftentimes means at least 50 percent. Therefore, if someone has racked up a large 401(K), he or she should be aware that that money is in play for the other person in a divorce settlement. You can negotiate and trade assets in the discussion of property distribution but those assets are in play to be distributed to the other party. So, if I own a house and I want to give you the equity in the house in lieu of my 401(K), I can do that if the other party would accept it.

It is a good thing. I'm getting what I want. You are getting what you want. The only problem with that premise is judges don't do that. Judges divide in simplicity. If you can't agree upon the house, the judge will sell the house. If you can't agree upon distribution of the assets, the judge will pick it. You may not like it. It's much better to try to enter into an agreement where everybody gets what they envision to be their fair deal; to pick the assets they want.

The Role Of An Order Of Protection In A Divorce Proceeding

Most divorces deal with children and with the allocation agreements today. The children are better protected than they were in the past and the parties have less animosity than they did in the past. Sometimes you have a very dysfunctional relationship and you need what's called an Order of Protection. An order of protection is very serious. It precludes a person from entering his or her own house and requires you to stay a certain distance away from the person who filed it.

An order of protection can be valid for 21 days initially; no notice needs to be given to the other side before you get it. However, because of urgent needs, an order of protection could last for 3 months, 6 months, up to 2 years or anything in-between according to the court. An order of protection can be modified once is has been entered. However, it is difficult to deal with when one is filed against you. You are essentially kicked out of your house and now you have to find a place to live. You can't go back in your house and get your things without a court order.

The rules of our court allow an attorney to come back in within two days of being served with an order of protection for their client. They don't have to wait to 21 days for a hearing, which a lot of people are not aware of. They can demand on within two days.

The Role Of Protective Orders In A Divorce Proceeding

Protective orders are another tool that attorneys sometimes use as a ploy to try to get possession of the children before a case begins. The reason behind this is so that they can litigate the case holding onto the children thinking that they can make this into a custody argument. Oftentimes, it doesn't work; it's not the function of an order of protection to predetermine custody. The function of the order of protection is to give some protection and peace of mind to the party seeking it. The person cannot come around, cannot contact them, cannot text message and cannot call.

The Role Of A Restraining Order In A Divorce Case

A restraining order has no duration of time. It lasts as long as the case lasts, or until further court order. Restraining orders can be very specific. The reason why is because if you violate a court order, the remedy is contempt. When you are held in contempt, if you violate a restraining order, there is no bail. There is no appeal. You sit in jail as long as the judge wants you to. Violation of restraining order is very drastic and it has immediate consequences.

Sometimes you have a very dysfunctional relationship and you need what's called an Order of Protection. An order of protection is very serious. It precludes a person from entering his or her own house and requires you to stay a certain distance away from the person who filed it.

Procedural Issues In A Divorce Proceeding

The other issues in a divorce are the procedural issues. You file a divorce where you are saying I want a divorce and the other person has 30 days to answer it. Once they answer it, you are now at issue. Two months after you file for divorce, there is something called a 218 conference. This 218 conference procedurally is when all dates are set; trial date, a pretrial date, the trial conference, discovery cutoff, expert disclosures and witness disclosures. From that point on, the judge sees you once a month to find out how you are developing in your plan of divorce and if you need assistance.

In Illinois, each county requires a parenting class to be completed. A parenting class is done in Lake County College for $75 and it is one evening where parties can go together. The court will require a completion certificate before he'll divorce you and usually want it before the parenting plan is entered.

College of Lake County has information online at their website to get that information to sign up for the classes and parties should do that when they file for divorce and get that part over with. The trial dates are normally in Lake County and many other jurisdictions such as Cook

County. They are usually written in stone so those trial dates should be expected to be adhered to.

Very few cases in divorce, believe it or not, end up at trial. Most cases are able to be resolved and the reason for that is a pretrial. Divorce cases are done by a judge, not a jury and you have an opportunity or your attorney does at least, to go before that judge in a pretrial and tell them what you think the case is about, what you want and why you think it's fair. The judge will chime in and try to help the two parties get to an agreement, almost like the mediation. You just tell them what you want to agree to.

Once the judge gives his opinion on what he wants to happen, you are now at the point where you have heard from the person who's going to be making the decision on your case. You would be a fool to go to trial at that point because you already know what he is going to say. Why spend the money unless you are looking for an appeal, or unless the judge missed something on one of those rare occurrences. However, most of the time, the judge will keep the same opinion at the time of trial as he does at the time of pre-trial.

Where cases do get to trial are those involving money, family businesses, evaluations of the business, evaluations of pieces of property, needs of maintenance and dissipation of assets. Dissipation of assets is a term that under the new law where you can only go back five years from when you were married to where the dissipation occurred, the marriage was falling apart. So for example, let's say you decided to get rid of money, maybe you gave it to your brother, maybe you gave it to your girlfriend, maybe you decided to spend money crazily or maybe decided to gamble it away. That's called dissipation, and it's a bad thing.

If you do it, you can expect the judge to catch on pretty quickly and to order it back into the marriage by taking it from your assets that you would be awarded. Often it will then be given to your spouse. That's dissipation of assets. It's very important to understand that those cases involve accounting, documents, a great deal of evidence and can get costly. It's really an accounting nightmare.

Trust Issues Between Estranged Spouses In A Divorce

Most cases don't have dissipation and most cases don't have valuation problems. Most cases just have arguments between a husband and a wife. What people should realize when they are getting a divorce and they are hiring an attorney is that the attorney is their best friend at this point. The attorney has the protection of their client in their mind and the best interest of the children. If they are a good practitioner, that's what they are thinking about. The problem is people have to realize when they are going through a divorce, they can no longer trust their spouse. He or she at that point in time has every interest to protect themselves, to protect their assets, to get their way and not to do what is in your best interest.

As a result, when a person files a divorce, I often tell them this is the time to separate your assets. You should separate your assets not to take them as you will have to account for every dime of it. But do so, to make sure the other spouse doesn't take them and give an exorbitant amount of money to another attorney to delay the case so that it costs more in the end. For example, let's say there is $50,000 hanging in a bank account, your spouse could take it all so go ahead and take it. The judge will understand. You will come into court with your bank deposit showing the money is now here. The court will instruct as to what to do; whether to keep it there or divide it. It's better to be safe than sorry. People often say, "Well,

I have a good relationship with my wife." However, they think about it overnight and when they go to the bank in the morning, they find out the wife has taken every last cent.

A competent attorney has their client do this so that they have control. The attorney knows if they dissipate it will cause more problems. If the other side does that, then the attorney has to go after them to get the accounting and that costs money. It's much better for the attorney to have control so he or she could direct the case and say to the other attorney, "Hey, no problem, here it is. It will be here in my client's account. We will do whatever we need to do. We are not taking it. We are preserving it."

It's legal. It's proper. It is protectionism itself, and there's nothing wrong with it unless you start dissipating it.

Another thing a person can do in preparation of a divorce is to get all financial documents including tax returns, bank statements, etc. in order. It's cheaper for you to bring it to an attorney than it is for an attorney to go get it. It takes a lot of effort to issue subpoenas and have them served when the information is just sitting on the kitchen table or in a drawer in your home. It's important to get that information because financial information tells a lot about the marriage's financial strengths.

Remember an attorney is not involved in the boyfriend/girlfriend aspect of a divorce, nor is the judge. What the attorney is involved in is the partnership of the business, splitting up the assets, getting each party to do a fair share and protecting the children who shouldn't be involved in any way, shape or form. They did not cause the divorce and were not party to it and neither parent should put pressure on the children.

The other thing a person can do in preparation for a divorce is to make a list of all assets and put values on them. Did you know it is free of charge to get a market analysis on the value of your house? When you

show that information to the other side, then there is nothing to argue about. They will see the value and see the comparable; if it's a $325,000 house on its best day and a $290,000 house on its worst day why not split the difference. That's how it works in real life. Those are important things to know when you get through a divorce and having a market analysis on the house is very helpful to the attorney. It gives them the value of the assets. It also shortens the divorce.

Selling a house during a divorce cannot be done unless you have a court order and have an agreement with the other side. Absent an order of protection, nobody could kick the other side out of the house during a divorce. Each party has the right to live there. As a matter of fact, our support statute says that a party, while they are going through the divorce, must be kept in the same standard of living that they have grown accustomed to. If the wife or the husband is the bread earner, or if they get their hair cut twice a week or colored once a month, they get to do that and you can't cut them off. If they took a trip to Paris once a year, they get to do that too. They do not diminish their lifestyle because a divorce is filed. People don't realize that.

> Remember an attorney is not involved in the boyfriend/girlfriend aspect of a divorce, nor is the judge. What the attorney is involved in is the partnership of the business, splitting up the assets, getting each party to do a fair share and protecting the children who shouldn't be involved in any way, shape or form.

MAINTENANCE OF THE STANDARD OF LIVING IN A DIVORCE

You are to keep the same standard of living that you have grown accustomed to during the marriage while the divorce is pending. When the divorce is over, then the standard of living can change. The issue on maintenance is what is called Alimony Maintenance in Illinois and it is financial support from one spouse to another. Two years ago, they created a statute and a guideline which solves most of the issues of maintenance at least in determining what it is.

Simply put, maintenance is 30% of someone's gross pay before tax. So if you make $150,000, 30% of that, is $50,000 or so. It would then be 30% percent minus 20% of the other spouse's pay. So if the other spouse earns $40,000, you take $8,000 off of the maintenance: 30 minus 20 equals what the maintenance would be.

There was a case recently where a couple claimed they had a rental property. We argued successfully to the judge that we didn't care if it was a business; it's still 30% of the gross. Even though they have to pay real estate taxes and pay maintenance on the property, the statute says, that's 30% of the gross and you don't deduct those things.

The other side skillfully argued they should deduct it because it's really not what he's getting. As maintenance is based on a deduction to the payer and a credit to the payee who has to pay taxes on it; it's based on the gross and not the net.

The statute also addresses the length of time someone will receive maintenance. It says that for 0 to 5 years of marriage, you will get maintenance for 20% of the time you were married. If you were married 5 years, you would get one year of maintenance. If you were married from 5 to 10 years, it's 40% of the time you were married and from 10 to 15 years, it's 60%. If you were married 15 to 20 years, you would receive maintenance for 80% of the marriage and then if it's over 20 years, the court will consider permanent maintenance for the length of the marriage.

If you are married for 30 years, you might get permanent maintenance or at least 30 years of maintenance. That's a tough boat to row because there have been many clients who we have successfully negotiated for where we gave up some assets because my client had been married for 30 years and didn't want to pay maintenance for another 30. We made a deal to pay for 5 years on maintenance and gave the wife more assets. Then she waived maintenance and we made a set number that was less than the 30 minus 20 and we allowed them to achieve an amicable result that helped both parties in the case.

These guidelines are a useful tool but it's not until you get before a judge that they become real. The judge will follow the guidelines; parties don't have to. Parties can do anything they want as long as it's fair and equitable; the court decides whether it's fair and equitable ultimately at the finalization of the case. Fair and equitable is a term of art. An attorney with 37, soon to be 38 years of experience would certainly know what's fair and equitable in a lifetime of experience viewing all kinds of cases.

The goal in a divorce case is to try to get the parties to an amicable resolution in their case, to facilitate parent and child relationships and to prevent abuse to a child or to a household member. When the case does not deal with children, it does not mean it's that much easier because people who used to go to bed with each other at night and were close to each other now can't trust each other.

Benefits Of Retaining An Attorney For A Divorce Proceeding

A good attorney is a guide through the system; not an impediment. A good attorney tries to get the case resolved, not to stonewall it and stop it from occurring. We have been involved in many cases where there were attorneys that tried to stop the case from proceeding for whatever motivation they had.

When there is a situation where there might be a problem with an attorney and we can't resolve it by ourselves, we bring it to the judge and tell him what's going on. Oftentimes that will get a case resolved. Though we have tried and won many cases the problem is that for your clients' best interest, it oftentimes is better not to try a case.

It puts a lot of aggravation, a time commitment and a lot of money from the client to try a case. If you can avoid it, you are doing your client a blessing. There are methodologies like mediation and pre-trials and 4-way conferences with the other side to resolve the case versus going to trial if at all possible.

As soon as we get a case, we start working on a settlement agreement. Once the case has been vetted, everybody knows what everything is, then it's time you to settle a case to avoid bringing it the great costs and expenses that can occur in drawing a case out.

> A good attorney is a guide through the system; not an impediment. A good attorney tries to get the case resolved, not to stonewall it and stop it from occurring.

Potential Costs Incurred In A Divorce Proceeding

People want to know how much a divorce is going to cost. The bottom line is that the cost depends heavily on how long you want it to go on for. That's how long it costs!

If you can get a divorce resolved sooner rather than later, it costs less money. However, most divorce cases take at least 20 hours. There are petitions, motions for support and motions for interrogatories to go through. There are also notices to produce, document review and by the time you are done with all that, there is a minimum 20 hours of time involved in the case.

The issue today is that we have a new law and we have different aspects of the law. All the old cases that interpret the old law cannot be used; all the old forms that interpret the old law cannot be used.

We have things in the new law such as right of first refusal. An example might be where a wife has to work late and would normally take the child to a babysitter.

However, under the new law she must give the husband the first right of refusal to take the child.

You also used to be able to live anywhere in Illinois you wanted. With the change in the law, now you cannot live more than 25 miles from where you lived before the divorce without court permission. You can now, however, go across the border as long as it is within the 25 miles.

> People want to know how much a divorce is going to cost. The bottom line is that the cost depends heavily on how long you want it to go on for. That's how long it costs!

Issues With Collaborative Agreements & Uncontested Divorce

We have had many people ask us about collaboration agreements and uncontested ways of getting a divorce done. The problem with those is that when one person is pushing for a collaborative approach, they are usually hiding something. A perfect example is when Attorney Bell handled a divorce for a woman and her spouse wanted a collaborative divorce which basically meant that they were not going to use an attorney.

The problem was that he gave her a list and his pension showed it was about $120,000. She was wary about that but it did show $120,000. It turned out that it was his donation to his pension and his actual was worth one million three. He was going to try to do a collaborative approach to hide it from her.

That discovery changed the whole tide of the divorce. She ended up getting the house, the vacation home and a lot of other properties and basically wrote her own ticket because she wanted to keep his pension. When we evaluated the 1.3 million, it's more than that ultimately when it pays out a number of years from now. So it was a fair resolve but it would not have been had she gone with the collaborative method. There is nothing wrong with folks saying we don't have a lot to dispute so let's go with one attorney. However, one attorney can only represent one party; he cannot represent both.

> We have had many people ask us about collaboration agreements and uncontested ways of getting a divorce done. The problem with those is that when one person is pushing for a collaborative approach, they are usually hiding something.

ADVANTAGES AND DISADVANTAGES OF FILING A DIVORCE FIRST

There is only one advantage to filing for divorce first and it is a tremendous advantage; choosing the forum. If you file a case, you choose what courtroom that case is going to be heard in. For example, if you are in Lake County and you don't want to litigate it downtown because it is a lot more convenient. So if you file first, that's where the case is going to be heard.

However, if you're not filing first, then there is no advantage because that means they just proceed first to trial. Sometimes going second at trial is a better strategy. When you go first, you present your case first. When you go second, you present yourself second.

But we do file a counter complaint because you could get through the whole case and the judge could rule in your favor on everything and all the other side has to do is dismiss it and then the case is over. So, if you don't have a counter petition filed, they can do that.

In the event you have a counter-petition it keeps the case live. They can't dismiss their case because you would just proceed on yours. Filing first is something of a quandary; it's a good idea so that nobody picks a lawyer from another jurisdiction and files it there. They will take the money. Chicago will take the money, Downtown attorneys will take the money and a Lake County Court will be deprived of the case. You will have to go downtown and fight to move it and pay the money to transfer it. So, it's better to file first and get your venue.

Potential Timeframe For Resolution Of A Divorce

The first question in a divorce after the case is filed is, "Now what? What do we do now? What about support? What about maintenance?"

What a person needs is true stability. They need to pay the mortgage, the electric bill and for the cars and they need some money for food, the children, etc. There just needs to be an agreement about the bills and to create stability.

A divorce process can take as little as 3 months, though oftentimes 6 months on a contested matter, but no more than 14 months usually. The judge has the case on their trial docket and they're not going to continue it, so that's the do or die date.

That's the date where a woman could say to her husband, "Do you really want that judge to make a decision on our lives?", or the husband could say to the wife, "Do you really want the judge to decide all of our issues regarding our children and other things?"

The parties should make their own decision with the guidance of their attorneys and the input of the judge. Don't let the judge make the final decision if you can avoid it. You see, the problem is not every family lawyer is trained in areas other than family law. In my opinion, it's just too limited to be just about family law even though that's what you are practicing. There are so many other areas of law to be familiar with; contract law, tort law, financial law, banking law and tax law. You need to be involved in a lot of areas of the law to be a good family law practitioner to do justice to for client. That is why you need to find the family practitioner who is engaged in many different areas of law so he can use all of that as a resource to guide you through this process.

> The first question in a divorce after the case is filed is, "Now what? What do we do now? What about support? What about maintenance?"

Handling A Contentious Divorce Proceeding In Illinois

Some divorces are contentious. The spouses don't like each other. They want to call each other names. They want to hire what we call a "shark". They want someone to beat up their opponent. Instead of going for a shark, people should consider somebody who is a problem solver. There are thousands of ways to settle a case but there may be only two or three ways that work for the particular parties. The job is to figure out what that is and propose it so an acceptable resolution can be achieved.

Attorney Bell once saw an attorney call the other party names. He felt that if he was doing that dog and pony show for his client, he's not doing his client justice. The client slapped him on the back saying "Hey, Way to go! You told her," but the problem is what did he accomplish? He alienated his only partner in settling the case. You can argue with your partner and you can show the partner where they are wrong. However, you should never treat them with disrespect. That's the difference. At the end of the day, the parties will be before the court proving their case, hopefully smiling that they finally got it resolved.

It is also a hope that you also did so within the realm of reason of legal fees so that both parties were not injured by that as well. Again, the parties are, believe it or not, in control of a lot of their legal fees. Each party has the burden of preparing their own case the way they deem fit. If you can't resolve the case, you will go to trial and the judge will make the decision.

It's a skilled divorce attorney that can avoid such a result and get a decision that their client asked for, wanted and is happy with.

Also, don't ever hesitate to enforce your agreement. A contempt issue can always be resolved, always negotiated. Creative thinking or thinking out of the box thinking is wonderful.

For example, there was a guy who could not pay the required maintenance as well as his child support. He was under water but he had equity in his home. With creative thinking, he was able to get a home equity loan, refinanced his house and now he prepays child support. The child support was non-deductible whereas the home equity loan was. So they

converted a non-deductible to a deductible item so the government pays one-third of that child's support payment it all being done this way. Now he doesn't have to pay any money directly to the ex-wife and has 10 years to pay off the home equity loan in the end the child gets the full benefit of the payment.

Sometimes people just try to satisfy that by taking out a student loan and co-signing it with your child but they will be had for child college expenses more often than not. Times are changing!

We had a case once where the man promised to pay for all the college and he became an actuary but he lost his job. He paid for the college but the child wanted to become a pilot and wanted to take an aviation degree. He got his first semester bill for gasoline and it was $30,000 a semester for gasoline to fly to friendly skies of North Dakota.

The judge said it's college expense; it's part of the lab fee. We took it up on appeal, the appellate court said that the father said all college expenses. That is an expense for college, it isn't coming from anywhere else. He has got to pay it. He said that he couldn't afford it and the appellate court remanded it back down and the judge found he couldn't afford it. The judge reversed himself and the judge took away the obligation to pay for that expense for school.

Nothing is black and white. Everything is grey in law. People try to fit the law to different circumstances, which is like taking a square peg and fitting it in a round hole. You might get it to fit but it'll be splintered all up and it doesn't look pretty. That's how the law is. People understand that we have rules and regulations but how does it apply to them? It applies to them supposedly like it's supposed to apply to everybody but in reality, everybody's facts and circumstances are different. Generically, you have a guideline of what should happen but things happen that are different because everybody's situation is different.

Nothing is black and white. Everything is grey in law. People try to fit the law to different circumstances, which is like taking a square peg and fitting it in a round hole. You might get it to fit but it'll be splintered all up and it doesn't look pretty. That's how the law is.

There will be an obligation of one party to pay child support and perhaps spousal maintenance. In Illinois, we have the uniform child custody act and that UCCA which is the ability to go after any father or mother who doesn't pay child support through the State's attorney and the county in which they reside or through a private attorney. It reaches across state lines now. They can grab the parent's tax refund. They can take away the parent's driver's license and you can get a judgment to cease assets from a bank account or have assets sold. That is called Enforcement of the Order.

When a party doesn't abide by a court order, we are back to the same issue of any court; it's contempt. When there is contempt, there has to be a purge ordered by the judge. The man is behind $10,000 in support, you hold them in contempt. Under Illinois statute, he will be liable for your attorney's fees. The amount is discretionary with the judge but he will have to reimburse for attorney's fees. When you go ahead and you hold them in contempt, the judge will sentence them to jail. To avoid going to jail, he has to pay $10,000 he owes you. That's the purge.

Once he pays $10,000, the contempt is wiped off and he also has to pay your attorney's fees. These agreements, the parenting agreements and the settlement agreements, are written with language in there because while they are agreements, they have become a court order!

When you violate the agreement, the contract, you violate the judge's order, you are in big trouble. You need an attorney to defend you or you could go to jail for a long time without bail and without appeal.

If you don't get the life insurance, it calls for and gives it to your spouse, you could be held in contempt. Anything you don't do in that agreement, you are held in contempt. If you do something you are not supposed to do like you come over to the person's house and demand to see the kids, you could be held in contempt. You fought long and hard for this agreement. You fought long and hard for the wording in the agreement and each and every word in the agreement. Shame on you if you don't use it to be enforced.

CONCLUSION

The purpose of this book is to give a general overview of Illinois and the changes in Illinois law for a person who is considering going through a divorce or who wants to know a little bit more about the divorce process. The purpose is also to understand that divorce is a dissolution of a partnership but there are personal feelings in the divorce and sometimes there are also in a partnership. For all those personal feelings, the parties should seek counseling to help them get through it. It is a dramatic event. You may have known this person your whole life or you may have only known them for a 6 months or a year, it really depends and every case is different.

What that means is that your life at this point in time is not normal, it is topsy-turvy. An attorney's job as a practitioner is to get it normalized, to know that your assets are not at risk, to know that you have support and income, to know that you are not going to lose everything that you had in your life in this divorce to either another spouse or to an attorney, to know that things will work out and tomorrow will be a brighter day! Tomorrow will be a day you will smile, and tomorrow will be the start of your whole new life!

Disclaimer

This publication is intended to be informational only. No legal advice is being given, and no attorney-client relationship is intended to be created by reading this material. If you are facing legal issues, whether criminal or civil, seek professional legal counsel to get your questions answered.

Ronald L. Bell & Associates P.C.
1113 S. Milwaukee Ave. Suite 204
Libertyville, IL 60048
(847) 495-6000
www.bestlakecountylawyer.com

Made in the USA
Monee, IL
05 November 2026

67386582R00036